Who is Madam Zucchini?

Doris Voss Dasenbrock (aka Madam Zucchini) spent many hours in the kitchen baking with her son when he was young. One of their favorite recipes was Aunt Vicki's Zucchini Bread. He loved to be in the kitchen to "help mix it." He started calling her "Madam Zucchini" whenever they would bake, no matter what they were making. Still she is called Madam Zucchini when baking or cooking in the kitchen. You can find the family favorite Zucchini Bread recipe on her web site:

www.madamzucchini.com

Forward

This is a poem story called, "Butterfly, Butterfly, What's Your Game Plan?" It is a descriptive, factual, and somewhat scientific look at the life of butterflies. It describes their whimsical nature, their manner of comings and goings, and the danger they sometimes find themselves in. It incorporates and illustrates the four stages in the life cycle of these beautiful, fanciful, fragile and capricious living creatures.

The butterfly poem is an observational commentary told in flowing, non-conforming rhyming verses. The story introduces many questions that are answered in a light, fun way that provokes one to do research to find out more scientific facts about these quixotic fliers that capture our fancy. An upper grade level vocabulary is used to expand the reader's knowledge in an informative, and imaginative way. Some words may need explanations and/or a dictionary. It intermeshes English poetry and the Science of Arthropods-Insects (Lepidoptera-Butterflies and Moths) in a unique manner.

The numerous illustrations show a variety of types of butterflies in their environments which help define the butterfly life story visually. They are rendered in watercolor and ink in rich colors in a controlled style to be more accurate. Other poem stories are rendered in a loose, more free form style to suit the myriad of subjects that happen to come into *The Garden of Surprises*.

Lotus Pond in *The Garden of Surprises*

Late Summer in *The Garden of Surprises*

Butterfly, Butterfly,
What's Your Game Plan?

Written & Illustrated by
Doris Voss Dasenbrock

Let's begin...
We have to have a serious talk, Butterfly.
We need a heart to heart, a frank discussion, you and I.
We need to converse about why I'm writing in poetic verse.
My statement will not be long, nor shall it be terse.
It is a bit unusual to speak to wild creatures in nature's wonderland.
It is not normally in our human nature; it's certainly nothing I ever planned.

Many people talk to their pets as if they can their chatter comprehend.
But who knows for sure the messages they really send?
There are some who think this type of behavior has "gone 'round the bend."
But Butterfly, not to worry, you can count on me as a friend.
I'll not capture you with a net, stick pins in your wings and put you on display.
You should be thoroughly studied, but not in that gruesome way.

When I talk to you, believe, on me you can depend.
I am still rational, I have not gone "off the deep end."
I 'm normal; I simply wanted you to know.
My talking to you is as natural as pure white snow.
I don't expect you to answer my questions in return.
They just help me create a pathway, your secrets to learn.

My strategy is to keep questioning until the answers I discern.
These questions won't keep you from your work, if that is your concern.
This process is called, "The Socratic Method," of which I doubt you have heard.
It is named after a Greek philosopher as a means to examine each word.
It is a way to learn true facts which promotes serious investigation.
It awakens the mind and stirs it to creative imagination.

Ideas need time for gestation and nurturing incubation.
Closely behind follows the gift of insight and then revelation.
Ideas once revealed can grow and bloom into an unexpected sensation.
Poor are the souls whose ideas are so few.
Poorer still if even those are ideas that are not new.
With searching and questioning, they could their minds grow.
If...they are willing to use their brains to read, think, learn, and sow.

Where did you come from Butterfly?
You didn't just one day drop out of the sky.
No, you had a mysterious beginning I would say.
Your physical shape didn't always appear this way.
In fact. you were rather ugly in your early youth.
It is a brutal fact, but it is the awful truth.

Your colors were different, your body too.
No one would suspect, that from your early age,
        there would be four of you, each in a different stage.
You had an unbelievable physical transformation.
It was life altering, and a reason for celebration!
To go from an egg, to a caterpillar, then into a chrysalis,
        and, *finally into a butterfly, is a unique revelation.*

Yes, you were a caterpillar only able to creep and crawl.
It took you forever just to scale a small wall.
Why? Because you were quite long and not very tall.
You were once a large, colorful worm-like creature.
But you turned into a butterfly with a wonderful feature.
You have wings to fly; you now have a bird's eye view from the sky.

What a transformation. *You are a totally new creation!*
From egg to caterpillar to chrysalis to butterfly, you're a sensation.
The four stages of life that you need to have, you pass quickly through.
You move through them so fast. I don't know, which is the REAL YOU?
Your secret is safe with me, only YOU know which is the best stage to be.
I only know that the one I prefer is the last; the one that's the best to see.

Butterfly, Butterfly, you seem to be willy-nilly fluttering.
As you flit about, are you also doing some muttering?
Zigzagging you fly effortlessly through the air.
You fly hither and yon, and over to there.
You fly with nary a concern or cautious care.
You dip and swoop landing, who knows where?

Do you know, can you tell where to land?
I've seen you sit down in the dirt and sand.
Certainly this seems to me to be not very well planned.
I don't think you are trying to get sun tanned!
When you sit in mud holes in groups, are you are socializing, sun basking, or huddling?
Butterfly experts explain your odd behavior as a need for mud puddling.

They tell us also that this strange habit is for a good reason.
It has to do with nutrition, your butterfly eggs, and the mating season.
They say that you draw water, salt and minerals from mud ponds.
In truth, I would much rather see you sitting on fern fronds.

Enough with the dirt, sand, mud holes and puddling!!!
Butterfly, come to my house and as you flit along your way,
        come mingle with my garden flowers, stay there, and "Make my day!"

Are you collecting drops of the fresh morning dew?
Are they from flowers that sparkle and glimmer too?
Or perhaps it's the raindrops that beckon to you,
    drops that have fallen onto petals like translucent pearls so new.
Whatever guides your work for the day,
    I'm sorry when you leave—I want you to stay!

In your everyday routine, I know you pollinate too.
That is good, because pollinators have become far too few.
You are heroic plant savers in your daily meandering operation.
You save whole species from extinction and thereby ruination.
Butterfly, how awesome is your job of pollination.
Why? Because you are responsible for our plant regeneration.

Selecting where to land and work requires much diversification.
You are to be thanked for your tireless work on landscape beautification.
Without accolades, praises, glory, hullabaloo, folderol or much ado,
    you quietly go about your daily work; work that is just waiting for you.
You are undaunted by the magnitude of vast fields needing your attention.
You know an overwhelming project is no reason for abstention.

That your work is indispensable is undeniably true.
Our beautiful gardens would be nothing without YOU!
But Butterfly, I do at times have to wonder,
        as I look up at you in the sky from down under.
Do you land happenstance on any old petal or leaf?
If by chance, it's poison ivy, does the itching cause you grief?

You are so diligent in your consistent work habits and dedication.
But I wonder Butterfly, just what is YOUR remuneration?
It must be the value YOU place upon your own work that you intuitively know.
That with time and patience, your beneficial value to nature will continue to grow.
The worth of your contribution is more than most people, even you, will ever know.
You are such a fragile, tiny creature, yet such a huge gift to us, you bestow.

What colors attract you, Butterfly?
What do you see from way up high in the sky?
Do you see bright yellows, oranges and reds?
Do their bright colors lure you into their flower beds?
Or, is it sweet nectar's aroma you seek as you flit and flutter by?
Perhaps its the variety of pungent fragrances that waft up so high.

Is it the size or the shape of each flower that has for you,
        the most compelling power?
What is it that catches your ever searching eye?
How do you make your selection as you helter-skelter espy?
Is it that which catches your fancy as you flutter by?
If you do pick out a dud, do you fly off for another try?

Are you swept up or down by a breeze?
Or, are you dithering along as you please?
Whenever the breezes or winds take hold,
        with a tail wind, you can become daring and bold.
You can be caught up in a swirling, whirling draft.
Luckily, *you are riding on your own aircraft!*

You are trying to maneuver yourself up, down, high, and low.
But your flights of fancy may take you wherever the winds blow.
Could there be a bird or insect sound that catches your ear,
      from down on the ground?
Something attracts you, what can it be?
Just why is it so difficult for us to see?

Could a butterfly, by another name,
    still be loved by all just the same?
Oleo Fly? Margarine Fly? Hydrogenated Oil Fly?
Should these strange names have been given a try?
Is any of these choices a suitable insect name?
If yes, would people love you, and your capriciousness, just the same?

"What's in a name? That which we call a rose, by any other name,
        would smell as sweet." Shakespeare's Romeo stated.
I guess he thought names were very much over-rated.
BUT…can a rose by another name be just as sweet,
        and just as beautiful to behold?
No, NO, not at all, this is what I have been told.

I think, NO, Never, Not by any such pseudo name,
        never, ever, Butterfly, would you any hearts attain.
You would have all your special attributes 'tis true.
But none of those substitute names would suit the real you.
You are an original, an unequaled sight in the sky.
You are the real McCoy; you are unique, Butterfly.

In far away places you have been seen flitting,
        dithering, skittering, resting and sitting.
You've gone into expansively large places,
        and into hilly green meadows' wide open spaces.
Beneath your wings are fields of wild flowers, clover, milkweeds,
        coneflowers, daisies, thistles and all manner of seeds.

I have noticed you, Butterfly, sitting with your wings spread out.
Are you drying them or are you collecting energy for your route?
Could you be storing up warmth into your body directly from the sun?
Are you like a solar panel pulling in energy for your daily run?
Is the sun providing you with fuel needed for a cross country trip?
Why do some of you take this mysterious long journey,
        "to give us the slip?"

Somehow Monarch Butterfly, long distances you know you have to go.
You don't hang around through winter's ice and snow.
With a chill in the air, you seasonally travel to the southern skies.
Are you intuitively flying by polar light that now catches your eyes?
You flitter and flutter with not even a GPS* as your guide.
You instinctively know this flight is going to be a lo-o-o-ng ride.

* Global Positioning System

Never a beeline, straight line or "as the crow flies" could you ever fly,
        even if you were to give a direct route, a serious try.
I believe meandering is a natural protection keeping you alive.
I think it is nature's way of helping you to survive.
You are safer fluttering in and out and all about,
        on your daily unexpected, undetermined circuitous, route.

Best to beware where you take your rest.
Choosing the highest place for you is best.
You can avoid a bad fate, a truly gruesome lot.
A lower location is where you should be NOT.
For you, it is definitely not the correct spot.
This is a warning, so I hope never to hear that you "forgot."

Butterfly, Butterfly, I admired you so.
You were spreading your wings on a flower, much too low.
You sat there, by the pond's edge where you ought not go.
This by my warning or instinct, I had hoped you would know.
Out in the water, a frog was sunning; he sat lurking, for a bite, just waiting.
That he hoped to be soon smacking his lips, there's no debating.

Butterfly, Butterfly, YOU put yourself in harm's way.
Now who knows HOW you will end this suspenseful day?
There are two possible outcomes I have to relate.
Hopefully you'll have one with a favorable fate.
One, of two destinies awaits you, for your unwise choice.
The first is a gruesome one to which I'll give voice.

This scenario goes like this—it is your undoing, your unhappy end.
No one can come to your aid, not even a friend:

    "Up popped that frog, I am sorry to say.
    He was to be the sad end to your sunny, fine day.
    If you thought frogs were slow and lazy, that was a bad hunch.
    In the blink of an eye, you easily became his gourmet lunch.
    His sticky tongue swooped you up in one tasty bite.
    Then sadly, you did not survive that May night!"

Thus ends your too short, lovely garden stay.
You left earth's picturesque playground in an unfortunate way.
There is no more fluttering high above the ground.
NO, you can't be resurrected; you can't turn your fate around!

Butterfly, Butterfly, you will be truly, sadly, sorely missed.
Because by a frog, you have been eaten, not merely kissed!
You will only live on through your eggs, your children to be.
But, there could be a different ending Butterfly, for us to see.
What if fate intervened, and gave you insight to flee from danger?
Flying out of harm's way, for you, would be a real "game changer."

What NOW is your destiny? Would you like to know?
This is a happier scene for you which I'm delighted to show:

"The frog leaped at you, but alas, he was a tad too late.
You flew away just in the nick of time; you escaped a cruel fate.
The frog now had to depend on another creature to be his meal.
For him, your fortunate getaway flight, was a very bad deal.
For once he leapt at any prey, he wanted its demise to seal.
Your ability to escape in flight, that frog would like to repeal."

Which of these two scenarios do YOU think happened that day in May?
You be the author, end this tale in your very own way. But, I will say,
both of these two creatures may have lived to see another day.
Be Advised: This ending is neither black nor white, but gray.

Butterfly Facts/Ficton To Check For Yourself:

1. Do butterflies taste with their feet?

2. Do butterflies live on only a liquid diet?

3. Do butterflies actually drink from mud puddles?

4. Why do butterflies spread their wings in the sun?

5. What is the life span of a butterfly?

6. What kind of eyesight do butterflies have?

7. Do butterflies hear noises and smell aromas?

8. What enemies do butterflies have?

9. What are butterfly wings made of?

10. How do butterflies protect themselves from prey?

Research Butterfly Notes

Dedication

My thanks go to my husband, David for technical assistance and encouragement, and our son, Derrick for critical feedback in reviewing this uniquely challenging project.

My thanks also to Alice Yeager, who teaches classes on designing and illustrating children's books. Her years of experience and individualized advice were very helpful in assisting me to work creatively, to look critically at my illustrations for consistency of style for this book series, and to deal with story content and the many other steps necessary to get this book printed and into the hands of readers.

Lastly, I wish to thank Craig L. Sparks, Chorale Director for the Bowie Senior Chorale for inspiring me to write poems. I found I enjoyed it tremendously and it has been a joy to continue writing with the added dimension of illustrating to complete the work as I envisioned the poem stories unfolding.

About the Writer/Illustrator

Doris Voss Dasenbrock, the author & illustrator of this publication holds a Bachelor's degree with a major in Art Education and a minor in English from the University of Wisconsin, Oshkosh. She holds an MFA degree from Florida State University, Tallahassee. She majored in fine arts, drawing and painting with a minor in the humanities. She also holds a marketing degree from the University of Maryland, University College, College Park.

She has taught art at all levels from elementary to high school, as well as night school adult classes in Wisconsin. In Florida, Maryland and Virginia she has taught college art classes.

She has worked commercially as a graphic artist, and as an advertising, marketing, and art director for a number of non-profit organizations and businesses located in the greater Washington, DC. area.

She has traveled to many countries in Europe, Africa, Central, South, and North America, Asia and Pacific Islands. She has taken countless photos and currently writes, illustrates and paints. Her art work has won numerous prizes and has been exhibited and purchased by both galleries and private collections nationally.

www.ingramcontent.com/pod-product-compliance
Lightning Source LLC
Chambersburg PA
CBHW042117040426
42449CB00002B/79